The Countryman's Britain in Pictures

A stockman in 1961. Note the
ubiquitous sack tied round his middle
to keep off the rub—and the cold.

The Countryman's Britain in Pictures

Crispin Gill

David & Charles
Newton Abbot · London · North Pomfret (Vt) · Vancouver

ISBN 0 7153 7450 8
Library of Congress Catalog Card Number 77-89381

Set in Ehrhardt by Ronset Limited Darwen
and printed in Great Britain
by Biddles Limited Guildford
for David & Charles (Publishers) Limited
Brunel House   Newton Abbot   Devon

Published in the United States of America
by David & Charles Inc
North Pomfret   Vermont 05053   USA

Published in Canada
by Douglas David & Charles Limited
1875 Welch Street   North Vancouver   BC

Contents

Introduction: Who Saw Him Die? 7

At Work 14

At Home 38

At Play 58

The Countryside at Risk 76

Chronology 94

Index 96

Acknowledgements

Alan Smith of the John Topham Picture Library found most of the photographs for this book. My wife Betty has been a zealous research assistant, my secretary Cynthia Margetts chased endless little facts and produced the fair copy, and my assistant Stuart Seager hunted out the last elusive pictures. My deep gratitude to them, and all the people who answered our questions.

My thanks to the following, for permission to reproduce their photographs: Harold Bastin (13, 22, 23), M. A. Booth (62), CoSIRA (26), *The Countryman* (39), CPRE (5, 29, 30, 47, 75, 78, 92), CTC (4), G. G. Garland (67), John Gaunt (58), *Home and Country* (68), Joan Lyne (34), Nicholas Napier (53), National Trust for Scotland (45), Peak Planning Board (9), Michael Richards, RSPB (90), Kenneth Scowen (35), Stuart Seager (61, 89), YHA (85). The rest are the work of John Topham.

John Topham

John Topham began work as a policeman in the East End of London, found photography took more and more of his time, turned professional freelance in 1933 and did not retire until 1973. Now he lives quietly in a remote cottage in West Kent, a little lame but still lively and working on his photographs. Apart from a sharp eye for a news picture he has, as his work in these pages shows, always been a first-class photographer.

The main dates in the chronology at the back of the book were taken from: *Agricultural Records AD 220-1968*, by J. M. Stratton (John Baker, London, 1969)
The Survival of the English Countryside, by Victor Bonham-Carter (Hodder & Stoughton, London 1971)
The Countryman's Britain, Editor Crispin Gill (David & Charles, Newton Abbot, 1975)

Introduction: Who Saw Him Die?

Revolutions do not happen overnight. The last sixty years have brought as many changes in the British countryside as the seventeenth-century enclosures in middle England, or the fourteenth-century Black Death. They have not happened all at once, or in the same place, or in different places at the same speed. We who have lived through these years have hardly seen them happening. In the same way the people of Petrograd could not wake up on one particular morning in 1917 and say 'this is the revolution'. It has like all revolutions been an accelerating process, getting faster as the years have gone by. We have to look back at old pictures to realise how the countryside has changed visually. We have to listen to the noise of the power saws and the tractors and the road across the way, the aircraft in the sky, to realise that the roar of machines has replaced the distant whistle of the train and the crowing of the cock in the farmyard.

In our time farming, the prime occupation of the countryside, has moved out of the depression that sat on the land from 1870 until the early 1930s into the energy age. The countryman has moved into the twentieth century in his way of life. The land is no longer worked by the muscle power of him and his horse. His horizons are no longer bounded by the country newspaper, the occasional visit to the nearest market town. The countryside has become the townsman's recreation, his dream life. We all babble of green fields. We have at last digested the message of Wordsworth and the early romantics and their endless successors in country writing. We all love the countryside, and writing books about it has become an industry in itself. 'Country fresh', 'country flavour', 'country means all you ever dreamed of'; the ad-man's message comes up every fifteen minutes on the TV screen. There are more of us too, many more, crowding one little group of islands, all better off and wanting more than we ever used to want.

All the changes have been meant well, intended for our betterment. Most of them have had unintended side effects. We have gained much. We live in greater comfort with more luxuries, more freedom. We have lost too, and a balance sheet, a profit and loss account is not easily drawn up.

The rural areas, from the intensive market gardens near the towns to the thinly-populated livestock rearing hills, grow our food. What is grown, how it is grown, has created the landscape around us. Even the rough country we call wilderness would look different if it were not grazed. Farming today is highly efficient, producing more food and (until the latest wave of inflation) bringing better rewards to the landowner and the farmer than ever before. His employee is better paid, works regulated hours, has paid holidays, lives in better housing. Neither he nor his wife is worn out with drudgery; they are better educated and their children go to better schools. There is the in-between class of family farmer where no labour is employed and the farm is small, on poor land, who have fared less well, but they are still better off than they were.

Farming has become mechanised, and machines want space, bigger fields.

So hedges have come down right through the lowlands, and in the corn-growing areas the old enclosures have given way to a prairie-like landscape. The hedges that survive are stripped of trees, because they get in the way of the mechanical hedgecutters which leave them as trim as suburban privet. Crops and beasts have to be disease-free, so farmers do not want strange feet in their fields, and footpaths disappear. The walkers find the roads intolerable and fight to keep the footpaths, though they existed originally for rural convenience rather than the new recreation.

Apart from the cars on the roads, all sorts of lorries want to get to the farms, and the farming machines must move about. So country lanes built for pack horses have to be widened, and road hedges give way to wire fences or post and rail. At least one can see through them, and not walk in a green tunnel. Metal gates are cheaper than wood, though less happy to lean on.

On the farm itself the old barns and outbuildings are picturesque but no longer efficient. They do not fit the new machines, and the storage needs have changed. Animals have new-style housing, milking is mechanised and must be hygienic. Silage towers sprout, singly and in clumps, of shiny metal or strangely painted. Hugh Dalton's post-war planning acts deliberately excluded most farm buildings from controls and dreadful things have resulted. Some highly efficient farms look like the factories they have become.

In the hills farmers want to improve their grazing, and again keep out disease. Even Snowdonia has endless wire enclosures and so much of Exmoor's heather has been ploughed that it may not be worth keeping as a national park. As late as the Hobhouse Report of 1947 it was proposed that

2 Lanefoot Farm, Troutbeck, between Windermere and the Kirkstone Pass in the Lake District; cutting hay in 1962. On these steep hillsides the horse teams have lingered on even into the late 1970s. Harvests come late in this hill country. 1962 was a catchy year; the tents of the August tourists can be seen in the meadow bottom right while Bob Thomson, the farm manager, drives his team.

8

the South Downs should become a national park. When the National Parks Commission came to designations there was not enough open land left to make it worth while as a park. Thirty years ago it was a tenet of the National Parks movement that good farming was the best guardian of the landscape. This is no longer true, and the Countryside Commission which has taken over the work of the National Parks Commission is currently exploring how efficient farming and good landscape management can be reconciled.

In 1918 most country dwellers relied on oil for lighting and cooking. A favoured few had electricity; even more, less fortunate, were on candles and wood fires. Now there are not many without electricity—or oil, or even gas, for central heating if they prefer. There is the telephone, radio, television in most cases. All this (and the demands of the towns) has meant orthodox power stations with their huge cooling towers, built like the chain along the Trent valley close to ample water supplies. After them came the huge bulk of nuclear power stations, again needing water and away from towns in case they leaked. The increased use of oil meant petroleum refineries, like that at Fawley in the New Forest, on the estuaries. Television meant transmitting aerials on lonely hills, and cats-cradle receiving aerials on every chimney. Telephones meant strings of wires along roadsides. Power meant pylons marching like giants across the fields. One has to see a wire-free village like Lacock, south of Chippenham, to realise what wires have done to our landscape. In recent years the Post Office, and even more slowly the Electricity Boards, have tried to tidy up sensitive areas. Where mains power cannot reach, domestic dynamos are available. Even a lonely island like Bryher in the Isles of Scilly buzzes of a night-time now like two dozen motor-cycles. All our villages have street lights so we do not have to wait for a full moon to visit friends. The view from any hilltop of a night now is of endless galaxies of sodium lights.

Villages have been given mains water and drainage, and the supply to lonely farms and cottages has been much improved. All this has increased the demand for more reservoirs which rob farmers of useful land in the lowlands and offend the conservationists in the hill country and the national parks. But we have more of both. Areas that avoid reservoirs by artesian wells are using so much that water tables are falling, to the distress of the rivers. Water piped to a house has to come out, drainage systems go into our rivers to add their pollution to that of industry and the waste products of battery farming that can no longer be used to fertilise the land. The chemical fertilisers and weedkillers used instead all help pollute the rivers. Against that real progress is being made to cleanse our waterways. There are salmon back in the Thames, and the Trent is cleaner than for decades.

The motor car, the most convenient form of personal transport ever devised, has been a boon to the countryman. But it has cut the railway system to a skeleton, killed coastal shipping and most of the canals. That in turn has cleared coastal harbours for yachting, and canals are being revived for pleasure boating. But road vehicles, and the increasing size of commercial lorries, are tearing the hearts out of villages that live on their routes, making life unbearable with noise and shaking old buildings to destruction. The remedy is to build motorways designed for the motor age, missing the villages, or by-passes. They in turn rip up the countryside along their routes and quarries get bigger and bigger as they produce the roadstone. With his car and the motorway even the modest driver can breakfast in Oxford and lunch in the Lake District. Millions of people can now reach the wilderness areas on a day out, to add to the pressure. Mountains have queues of orange-clad climbers all through the weekends.

Most people are more mobile, but another victim of the car has been the country bus. The large number of people who do not have cars, particularly the very young and the old, are more isolated than were their forebears fifty years ago. Car-owners can shop in the nearest town's supermarkets, and the loss of trade kills off the village shop, again to the detriment of the non-mobile. The village shopkeeper begins to disappear with the wheel-

wright, the blacksmith, and all the other tradesmen who serviced the old-style farming. Men have been leaving the land for a century now because of the low pay and conditions of work, so machines had to replace them. Machines are made in town factories and serviced from them, and the spiral effect removed more work from the villages.

Those country towns which have the shops and the services have had to widen their streets, find car parks, paint yellow lines and employ traffic wardens. The 'developers' have moved in, corn markets have become supermarkets, whole rows of old buildings have been ripped out to make new shopping precincts that might be anywhere. All our Market Streets begin to look the same.

The welfare state, that may be dated back to the Liberal landslide of 1906 but really began with the Attlee Government of 1946, has made life better in many ways. County hospitals, often rebuilt, are more efficient. Country general practitioners work in many cases from new health centres. Alms-houses are improved, old people's homes a world away from the union workhouses that survived into the 1920s. Unemployment pay, pensions, family allowances are all cushions against hard times. Against that many small towns have lost their cottage hospitals and in a world of few buses old people find it hard to get twenty miles to visit aged relations. Cottage

3 Ploughing on the South Downs, near Lewes, 1952. The Downs, once famous sheep runs, have been under pressure from the plough for a century now and the 1947 proposal to designate this area a National Park was abandoned later by the National Parks Commission because so little open land was left. 1952 was a good year; this ploughman (who today would by law have safety bars on his tractor in case he rolled over) is ploughing in the stubble right after the harvest. For years now stubble has been burnt off; this bleached landscape would have been a black desert.

hospitals that have survived are invaluable in their new role, a cross between health centre and geriatric ward.

Improving education with more centralisation has also meant a loss of village schools. The one-teacher school of the old type with a brilliant teacher was a wonderful institution, but such people are not common and the new system makes for more educational opportunities. Against that the child taken day after day by bus away from the village, and from an early age, loses that sense of belonging. The big world calls too soon. School buildings are sold up and villages left with no meeting place. The departed teacher is a lost leader. With its manpower shortages too the Church is amalgamating parishes, forming group ministries. Another natural leader is lost to the community, along with the village policeman who is increasingly based in the nearest town, leaving the villages in the care of motor patrols without local links and local knowledge.

All these new services have to be paid for out of taxation, and death duties have broken up many old estates. No more does the villager have to vote the way squire or farmer does, and touch his hat to the lady as she makes her charitable round. But another leader has gone. Where the big house survives it is probably open to the public. The National Trust may have moved in. Visiting stately homes is now a national sport and we can see treasures of architecture, furniture, paintings and gardening that once were preserved for the few. The employment available in service has gone too, but the open house does employ village people.

High taxation has seen two other rural developments; the industrialist who buys a farm and runs it as a hobby, setting his losses against his other profits; and the rich man who develops forestry as a way of investing money for his heirs that will escape death duties. Many acres of hardwoods have fallen before the blanketing spruce for people who may never have seen the land they invest in. Both these activities have been reduced in scale in recent years.

4 Cycling in the Yorkshire Dales National Park. These cycling club members are using Mastiles Lane, a green track high above Malham in some of the wildest moorland in Yorkshire. The cattle show that this is good stock-rearing country and the constant problem of national parks is to balance the preservation of the wilderness and natural beauty with the needs of recreation and the work of the native farmers.

The welfare state has also built new towns, and huge estates of new houses to clear the in-city slums, but they have sprawled out across the countryside, very often taking the best farm land. The farmers who find the new estates on their doorsteps have neighbours with no country knowledge or understanding. So the countryside shrinks, and between the farms and the streets develops a blighted no-man's-land. All this new building has brought endless gravel pits, particularly in the Home Counties and the Thames valley. Once exhausted they make good nature reserves or nice water sport centres, but the landscape looked better in its original state.

Yet we all love the countryside today. We appreciate its beauty, we are against litter, we cherish its old villages and fight for its old buildings. So more of us are getting out into the country, and need more facilities; cafes, restaurants, car parks, lavatories. They are no good if they cannot be found, particularly lavatories, so they cannot be too carefully tucked away even at the most sensitive beauty spot. Crowds attract ice cream vans, and wear out the turf and do make litter even when they mean not to. The more people get out, the harder solitude is to find, and cars get pushed into more and more remote corners to the detriment of grass tracks and the destruction of more solitude.

Townspeople want weekend cottages, that become retirement homes. The railway age enabled them to live further and further from the noisy towns, and the motor car has spread the commuter belt of every city further afield. So villages have their estates of 'Georgian-style houses' or sad bungalows on their outskirts. Other commuters and retired people move into old cottages and bring them up to modern standards. Against this it is accepted that the labour force needed in the countryside today is a quarter of what it was when the villages and market towns were established to house that labour force, and without the 'incomers' a large number of cottages would be empty and derelict. But in turn that puts up the price of old cottages in pretty villages, and the locals cannot afford them even when they want them. In turn again the locals probably lacked the capital for the improvements wanted.

The new capital in the country has improved the appearance enormously of many villages. The new people are the strongest defenders of the old beauties, very often the new leadership and driving force of the community. Not that it is always appreciated or welcomed; there is strain between 'us and them' most marked when nearly all the indigenous population is to be found in council houses on the edge of the village and the incomers occupy the cottages of their ancestors.

It was the uncontrolled spread of urbanism into the countryside in the 1920s, the ribbon development for instance, that led to the formation of the Council for the Preservation of Rural England in 1927 (the 'P' stands for 'Protection' now). That body cut its teeth in fighting against the Forestry Commission, notably in the Lake District in the 1930s and led to a much higher concern in that body for amenity values in doing its statutory and necessary duty of rebuilding our forests. The young walker was helped by the creation of the Youth Hostels Association in 1930 and the strengthening of the newly-named Ramblers Association in 1935. CPRE and RA laid the seeds for the creation of national parks in 1949 and Government concern for landscape, with national parks followed by areas of outstanding beauty, heritage coasts and the like. The concern for the whole countryside, not just the special areas, turned the Parks Commission into the Countryside Commission in 1968 and the voluntary Civic Trust, founded by Duncan Sandys in 1956, began to care for towns, large and small, as CPRE did the countryside. Innumerable local amenity societies were revitalised or reborn in these post-1946 years and the backbone of all of them were the new country dwellers, or the townsmen whose hearts and holidays were in the country. They were too the driving force in the new concern for nature and wild life. Bird-watching became a major pastime, nature trusts and nature reserves proliferated. Conservation has become a fashionable word.

So all should be well. In Whitehall we have a Department of the Environment to look after the countryside, and every county and district council has its planners to see that the details are right. But farming, which controls the essence of the landscape, is with the Ministry of Agriculture, Food and Fisheries. They give money to landowners to plough up moorland and put up wire fences, while the DoE and its agents try to keep the wild areas of the national parks as they are. The Forestry Commission is planting trees, and encouraging others with subsidies to do the same, and the two Countryside Commissions (Scotland has its own) want to keep open access land in the hills. Our Government speaks with two voices. The civil servants concerned have started talking to each other at last, but all they have worked out so far is where they disagree.

Outside government there are the rest of us, all country-lovers. The militants organised in their amenity societies think the farmers, the foresters, the road-builders, the quarrymen, the housing estate builders, are all vandals. In fact they are all bird-loving, picnicing, holiday-making, badger-watching followers of Wordsworth like the rest of us, but they also believe that their way of earning a living is vital to the well-being of the nation, of us all. We all want water, but the reservoirs ought not to be on our doorstep. We accept the need for rural industry, but no factories in our village, please. And so the arguments go on.

We have had the revolution. Farmers took two or three centuries to change their main motive power from the ox to the horse, and that had minimal impact on the rest of us. They have changed from four legs to four wheels in two or three decades. The first Ordnance Survey maps of about 1800 could still be used to get about the country in 1920. They can still be used to help work out the Domesday Book of William the Conqueror, but they are not much help to the 1970s traveller. A way of life that had persisted for centuries, with only infinitely slow changes, is dead. The revolution is not finished. Energy and everything else has stopped being cheap. Big may not be beautiful after all. Growth is not going on for ever. What do we do now?

The countryside, and our life in it, has been revolutionised in this century. A way of life unchanged for centuries is dead. We can list what we have gained, and what we have lost, but whether we show a profit or not is a matter of personal judgement. I would say that the land is better to work in, better to live in and, by and large, better to look at. If on balance we have gained, we must see that we hold those gains.

At Work

In past years those who dwelt in the
countryside have earned their living
there, either directly on the land like
the farmer and his men, or in the
trades that supported farming like the
wheelwright and the blacksmith, or
those who provided the necessities
for the rest of the community, like the
cobbler and the basket maker. Carters,
millers, drovers, railway men,
postmen, publicans; they were all
part of the country scene. Now
increasingly the men have to find their
work in the nearest town.

5   Court Farm yard, Chipping
Campden, Gloucestershire, in the
1920s. Agriculture and its ancillary
trades were the principal sources of
country employment, and the
farmyard its heart. This yard is in the
shadow of a great Perpendicular 'wool'
church founded on the fortunes of the
Cotswold sheep runs, and in front of
the nave can be seen the ogee-shaped
roofs of the gateway of the old manor,
destroyed in the Civil War. There are
still a few of its ruined buildings
behind the photographer on Dover
Hill, now National Trust property
and until 1851 the scene of the
Cotswold Games. In the farmyard
the dovecot and the slated lean-to
piggery below it have gone, as has the
wall and the thatched shed right. In
the 1920s a crippled Irishman who
lived in the almshouses across the
road and earned a living catching
rabbits and moles hung his skins to
dry under this thatch; his father first
came to Campden as a navvy building
the railway. The waggon in the yard is
typical of the elegant South Midlands
or Cotswold bow type, described
nearly two centuries ago as 'beyond
all argument the best farm wagon
. . . in the kingdom'. No farming is
done from the yard now.

6 The old tithe barn, Naseby, Northamptonshire, 1930. One of the finest barns in the county, 90ft long and 25ft wide, its oak pillars based on stone foundations and with lath and plaster in the upper part, it was in parlous state when this picture was taken in 1930 and eventually pulled down. All large old barns in England tend to be called 'tithe barns' though this was not built till after the Battle of Naseby in 1645 (which decided the outcome of the Civil War) and long after the dissolution of the monasteries, for which tithe barns were usually built. This barn dwarfs the farm machinery stored in it, and old farm buildings are constantly at risk as modern agriculture demands quite different buildings which can rarely be afforded in vernacular materials or styles.

7 Man power: a mower with his scythe, 1947. Fred Goldup is cutting the headland by scythe before the reaper and binder come into the field. The sacking cradle is to ensure that the corn falls in neat swathes ready for binding. A good man could mow an acre a day, but it was hard work, demanding much skill and a scythe constantly sharpened by the whetted stone or the strickle. The doles, or handles, on the snathe, or shaft, were adjusted so that a man could mow in the most comfortable position for his height. When gangs of mowers would reap a field in the days before machines the scythes would be provided by the farmer, but the labourer would use his own sickle.

8 Carlisle hiring fair, 1951. Until the 1920s it was common for men seeking new employment and farmers needing labourers to attend a hiring, or mop, fair, usually at Martinmass (late in November), where bargains were struck for a year's labour. In Carlisle the custom survived very late.

9 The milk donkey, 1961. Donkeys as beasts of burden supplemented man power, notably where sureness of foot was needed as on the potato patches in the Cornish cliffs, and still in the motor-free street of Clovelly in north Devon. This milk donkey, Jimmy, was carrying the milk in churns at Castle Bolton, North Yorkshire. Note the stile left; room for a man to pass when the gate was shut, but not an animal.

10 Ox cart on Fair Isle, 1949. From Celtic times until the seventeenth century oxen were the major motive power on farms right through Britain, but they were gradually replaced by horses, surviving longest in the loneliest corners. This ox cart was the last on Fair Isle. Mr William Leslie, leading the beast, grew cabbages, potatoes, oats and turnips on his 20-acre croft, kept a house cow and 22 sheep. The ox drew his plough as well as the cart. Once a week Mr Leslie met the mail boat with his cart and became the postman too.

12 Steam ploughing, 1920s. Steam brought early mechanisation to the farms and the engines, usually brought in by contractors, could be used for both ploughing and threshing. Because the engines were by their nature heavy, and compacted the land, they were commonly used in pairs for ploughing, one each side of the field and drawing the plough from side to side by cables from a drum under the engine. With the greater power more furrows could be cut. This balance plough has four shares each side, though six were common and eight possible. The photograph shows clearly how the side not in use was swung clear of the ground. The engine that was not hauling moved ahead to be ready for the next furrows.

11 Three horse team, 1938. A picture that epitomised prewar farming; massive horses straining to drag a spike harrow across the heavy soil. For generations the horse was the prime motive power and the straw from its stables manured the fields. It needed no expensive oil as fuel but ate three acres of oats each year and needed much care and maintenance. The horseman not only had to walk behind his team for most of the daylight hours but spend another four hours a day preparing the animals in the morning and grooming them at night. Still he was proud of his team and their turn-out; notice the brasses on these horses' heads.

13 Reaper and binder, early 1920s.
The boy in his Eton collar, straw
hat and knickerbockers is fascinated
by this sophisticated machine of the
horse age. One man with a pair of
horses cut the corn which the
revolving reel held against the knife
and then laid on the platform, whence
it was carried up over the master
wheel to be gathered into sheaves and
automatically bound before being
dropped. The master wheel drove all
the machinery involved, from the
revolving reel to the binder, through
an intricate system of gears and chains.
Men still had to follow the binder
and stook the sheaves.

14 Carrying a wartime harvest, Herefordshire, 1944. The internal combustion tractor from its beginnings about the turn of the century had a great impetus from World War I and became even more useful after the development of pneumatic tyres for them in 1932. This photograph of Bailey's Meadow at Hall Court, Much Marcle, near Ledbury in Herefordshire, shows the march of time. The binders have done their work, the sheaves have been stooked, and now the corn is being carried to the ricks near the farm. There are four tractors in this field alone, towing the hay carts. The one on the left has also been fitted with pneumatic tyres. Typical of the wartime years, five of the workers in the field are women; four of them on top of the carts stacking. Heaving up the sheaves by pitch-fork was hard going even for the men.

15 Combine harvesters, Wiltshire, 1964. Five combine harvesters in echelon sweep across the great fields of Salisbury Plain—in this case at Middle Woodford, Wiltshire, between Salisbury and Amesbury. These machines are reapers and threshers combined; the barley is pressed on the cutter bar by the reel and carried by elevators to a series of beaters and threshers. The grain drops into a pan and thence to a chaffer sieve which separates the grain from the chaff, which is thrown out behind the harvester with the straw. The grain is taken by elevator to a storage tank above. The tractor-drawn container collects the grain from each tank as it fills. Drivers of these machines find dust a problem. There are pictures of early models with the men wearing gas masks. Many modern combines have air-conditioned cabs. The British harvest was almost completely mechanised with binders by 1920; since World War II the combine has taken over until by 1970 there were over 60,000 in use.

16 Hill sheep in Scotland, 1964. The shepherd and his dog moving a flock on Sir Alec Douglas-Home's farm near Douglas, Lanarkshire, in what is now under local government reorganisation the Region of Strathclyde. This scene could be reproduced in most parts of Wales or any of the upland areas of England.

17　Dairy herd, Hampshire, 1965. A traditional scene but with a number of differences. The cattle are Friesians, the black and white breed originally from Holland which now yields 70 per cent of the milk produced in these islands. The farmyard has been cemented and has metal railings, and the path in from the field is flanked by electric fences. These fences are now used extensively to control grazing, so that a herd eats its way methodically across a pasture.

18　Cattle ranching and forestry, the Great Glen, 1960. Two-thirds of Scotland is in the Highlands, islands and uplands, and beef cattle the major product of Scottish agriculture. Since World War II cattle ranching has been developed on some of the large estates, notably in the Great Glen and as in this scene north of Fort William, photographed in 1960. Extensive forestry has been developed in the upland areas too, and the serried rows of conifers can be seen in the background on the lower slopes. Where it is reckoned that sheep need one man a thousand acres, forestry needs six. Ten per cent of Scotland's total area, or 2 million acres, is now taken up by forestry.

19 Potato lifting in north-east Scotland, 1963. Various corners of Britain have their specialised crops; from the rich but cold eastern areas of Scotland between the mountains and the sea come seed potatoes for the whole of Britain, and much of the main crop. These casual labourers are lifting Majestics on a five-acre field overlooking the Howe of the Mearns, near Fettercairn. 'Tatie-picking' is traditionally a part-time job for women; there are a number in this picture and one has her child perched in the furrow.

20 Broiler fowls in Lincolnshire, 1963. These table birds are being produced on Lord Burghley's estate at Stamford, Lincolnshire, in a controlled environment, automatically fed. There are few free-range birds in Britain today, either for egg producing or the table.

21 Hops in Kent, 1958. From Kent and East Sussex come two-thirds of the hops grown in England, with the rest coming from Herefordshire and Worcestershire. Both these areas grow fruit intensively as well, but modern machinery has largely replaced the old casual labour of gypsies and, in Kent, the holiday-making hop-pickers from east London. In this photograph of Nettlestead Farm, Paddock Wood, Kent, with the typical cowls of the oast houses in the background, Mr Jim North is pulling down the bines; he was a postman from Chiswick who had spent all his holidays since boyhood, apart from the war years, doing just this on the same farm.

28

22 Charcoal burning, early 1920s.
The dog with his barrel kennel, the fowls and the cooking pots suggest that these charcoal burners were following the old practice of living in the woods for days at a time. Making charcoal was a way of using the waste wood, above all in the coppiced oak woods, and supplied a fuel which has been needed since Roman times. Charcoal is still used commercially but it is produced now either from large metal cylinders in which the wood is burnt—still taken into the wood for the process—or else by factory methods where the side products, which used to be lost, can be collected. The last of the old-style charcoal burners probably finished about twenty or thirty years ago.

23 A bodger's camp in the Buckinghamshire woods, early 1920s.
In rough camps such as these in the Chiltern beech woods the bodgers with primitive but highly effective pole lathes—the poles can be seen projecting from a couple of the huts— turned from green beech the legs, spars and stretchers of the Windsor type chairs. The assembly was done in the nearby furniture towns such as High Wycombe and the bodgers would work in the wood from which they were getting their material, moving on when they had worked out a plantation. The last bodger stopped work some twenty years ago, and their turnery now is factory-produced.

24 Cornish wheelwright, 1956.
Mr J. C. Williams of Mawgan in Meneage, near Helston, has heated the iron tyre of a cart wheel to expand it, placed it over the rim and is watering it so that it does not burn the wood. The cooling contracts the tyre and holds the whole wheel together. The horse has come back for recreation but carts and waggons are little used; few wheelwrights remain today. Once, like so many crafts ancillary to the old-style farming, there was a wheelwright in almost every village.

25 The Old Forge, Groombridge, Sussex, early 1930s. A picture that almost tells the decline of a trade. Here the blacksmith is at work on a horse while he talks to the motorist; in village after village as the use of horses declined and the number of cars increased, so blacksmiths' shops became garages. Apart from going over to garage work the blacksmith also found his skills needed by the increasing use of machinery on the farms. In the years since World War II the growth in popularity of the horse for recreation has meant a strong revival in farriery. Many farriers nowadays have travelling workshops in light vans. The buildings in this picture, with their weather boarding and brick chimneys, are typical of much of Kent and East Sussex. In some places it was the old livery stables which gradually went over from horses to motor cars; in Burford for instance the Bridge Garage which closed in 1976 was owned by the family whose father had been coachman to the business operated from the temperance hotel which is now *The Countryman* office. When the hotel closed about 1909 the coachman started on his own; when his son took over he brought motor cars in. The temperance hotel had been a coaching inn in the late eighteenth century, so this Burford garage represented two centuries of transport history.

26 Thatching in Huntingdonshire, 1951. Thatching is another craft which began to fade after World War I; the reed was expensive, modern harvesting methods produced short straw from the cornfields, the roof was shorter-lived than those made of other materials, and the fire risk drove insurance premiums high. The Government set up a Rural Industries Bureau in 1921 to help employment in the country, launched a Rural Industries Loan Fund in 1940, and brought them together with the county organisers formerly employed by the Rural Community Council to create in 1970 the Council for Small Industries in Rural Areas (CoSIRA). The thatcher in this picture, Mr O. Seaman of Godmanchester, was one helped by these organisations. He is roofing council houses in Hemingford Abbots, near Huntingdon, with Norfolk reed. Many local authorities have carried out their obligations to replace the old rural slums with decent housing in the cheapest manner possible and far from improved the villages. Some authorities, however, have been at great pains to build in the traditional style of the village concerned. The village here, Hemingford Abbots on the Ouse, was predominantly thatched and not only the new council houses but the modern school was roofed accordingly.

27 Canterbury cattle market, 1936. In the early 1920s it was still common to see cattle on the hoof driven into the towns either for the market or the slaughter house. This picture shows how the old drovers were being replaced by lorry transport, although the farm cart is still in evidence. Markets produced work for auctioneers and their staffs, the dealers, the hauliers and for the shops and hotels of the town. Market days have always been a day out for farmers and their families. The men's hats in the picture almost show the social standing of the wearers, bowlers or trilbys for the employers, cloth caps for the workers.

28 Middleton in Teesdale railway station, 1952. Country railways were not only a great force in opening up rural areas in the pre-car days but were also important employers; the railway servants had a cachet and the pension attached to the job made it sought-after employment. But at this end-of-the-line Yorkshire station there were only six trains a day in 1952; the staff had time on their hands, and an enthusiastic gardener in the porter, Mr F. Crowther. For the five years before this picture was taken the station had won prizes as the best-kept and prettiest station in the North-Eastern Region. Inevitably perhaps it was closed under the Beeching axe of 1963.

29 The road across Reeth High Moor, above Feetham and Swaledale, about 1920. The village lengthman who looked after the roads of his parish was a wellknown character between the wars. Though tarmac was invented and first applied in 1904 and county councils had been responsible for road maintenance since their formation in 1888, little had been done even by the 1920s. This picture of an intrepid motorist crossing the Yorkshire Moors shows the road surface of the time. The roadmen would break up piles of stone beside the roads, fill potholes with large stones and tamp smaller and smaller stones into the hole to bind the material. Mud in winter, dust in summer, was the order of the day and the cause of much early fury against the motor cars which stirred up one or the other. Notice too that this driver has a gate to open round the next bend, and a watersplash at the bottom. Few roads survive with this coaching-age macadam surface, cattle grids have replaced gates and water splashes become so rare that conservationists fight to preserve them.

30 Newark Mill on the River Wey, Surrey, early 1920s. Inland waterways and mills were sources of employment well into modern times but large factory mills in the towns have almost completely replaced the small country flour mills, whether wind or water driven. This weather-boarded mill with its mansard roof, the greatest of the considerable number of Surrey mills, was remarkable for its three waterwheels. It was grinding corn until the late 1950s and then used as a store; its destruction by fire in 1966 was a considerable loss. By water it was only five miles from the Thames, and until 1871 was on a canal route that linked London with Portsmouth and the Channel. The River Wey is still navigable from the Thames to Guildford and by small craft for a few miles above. Now National Trust property, it is given over to pleasure craft.

31 Weather has always been a hazard for the country labourer; if he could not work he was not paid and so he struggled on if possible. These two men with a three horse team were ploughing during the blizzard winter of 1947.

32 Outer Hebrides postman, 1960. The country postman, by foot, bicycle, boat or, as with Donald MacDonald here on North Uist on horseback, has had to face all kinds of weather. Donald MacDonald changed horse for van in 1961, and is still the postman of North Uist.

33 The carter in rain, late 1920s. It is not flood water in the picture but a pond; carts and waggons were driven through water particularly in dry spells to make the wooden spokes and rims of the wheels swell and hold firmly together.

At Home

The hearth has always been the source of heat and the means of cooking, the focal point of mansion (which had many fires) and tiny cottage, in houses cramped together in market towns or scattered through the fields. The shops, the church and the school in their various ways have all supported home life. The great change of our times has been the arrival of mains services and modern conveniences to relieve the housewife of the old drudgery.

34 Beside the fire, Herefordshire, 1943. *The Countryman* for Summer 1943 identified the objects in the picture from left to right. Eighteenth-century spindle-back chair. Oven peel. Eighteenth-century firedogs. Victorian 'fountain' for continuous hot water, hanging from adjustable pothook. Seventeenth-century 'sway', which swings out. Eighteenth-century copper cooking pot. Oven below fire. Such fireplaces survived in many farmhouses until well after 1945, though they may have been supplemented by a small oil or portable gas stove in the scullery. It is not uncommon when modern fireplaces are taken out of old houses to find such open hearths behind, and the hooks and chains still in place.

35 Country town; Cirencester, 1970.
The largest parish church in
Gloucestershire dominates the splendid
market place, another Cotswold
'wool' church though the money for
its wonderful tower came from the
town's loyalty to Henry IV in the
struggles of York and Lancaster.
New good buildings have been added
to the market place over the centuries,
modern development has been kept
out of the centre, and in recent years
a Civic Trust street improvement
scheme has much brightened the
appearance. But if it were not market
day there would be cars in the centre
of the place and not stalls with their
awnings. Yellow lines control kerb-side
parking, and television aerials on the
skyline confuse the splendid pinnacles
of the church. The horse on the
bracket is an old sign of a saddlemaker.

36 The village complex:
Chiddingstone, west Kent, 1969. The
village school bottom left (a hundred
children in 1977), the church looking
across to a seventeenth-century village
street so perfect that the National
Trust acquired it in 1939 and it is still
used for television drama settings,
and the 'Castle' standing a little aloof
in its own grounds. The Streatfeild
family elevated their pleasant country
house into a 'castle' in the early
nineteenth century; the first
Streatfeild was an ironmaster who
made his fortune in the sixteenth
century from Wealden iron. The
family sold the castle before World
War II but still live nearby. Their
old home, like so many big houses,
is now open to the public, and in this
case houses a museum of armoury.

37 The lonely cottage, Timberton
Bottom, 1952. There have always
been farms and cottages scattered
through the countryside away from
the villages, difficult to provide with
modern services because of that
isolation. This cottage has a telephone,
and its occupants supplemented their
living by serving teas, but often these
isolated dwellings were the first to
be abandoned because of their
loneliness and lack of facilities. This
footpath is well trodden but in many
parts of the country they have
become a battleground between
farmers and walkers, notably led by
the Ramblers' Association. To
farmers the footpaths are a nuisance
in working their fields and their users
are not always well-behaved. To
walkers they are in lowland England
almost the only way of escaping the
roads and their traffic.

38 Wartime fireside in Sussex. The family gathered round the fire in this farmhouse near Cuckfield with their dogs look comfortable enough. The daggers over the fire (left) have an Arab feel; perhaps one of the men is home from the First Army in North Africa.

39 The wireless, 1927. Nothing ended the isolation of country life more surely than the arrival of wireless. Earphones, condensers, moving coils, batteries and accumulators all became part of everyday life in the 1920s. This cottage fireplace is on a less grand scale than the one above or that in photograph No 34, but its black-leaded stove was a great advance for cooking on the old open fire.

40 Water supply, 1939. If the work on the land was hard on the men, the drudgery of running a home without piped water, electricity or gas, and all the services and labour saving appliances that can come with them, was hard on the women. Many country districts were relying on wells and streams until well into the 1950s and some outlying places still tap their own sources. Rebecca Munday of Dean Bottom in Kent, at her only water supply in 1939, does not look to have had an easy life.

41 Peat in Shetland, 1957. Mrs Malcolmson of Quarff, just south of Lerwick, carrying peat home to dry in the 'keshie', a locally-made basket. Sticks and wood for the fire, gathered from the woods or the beaches, have never been despised by country people but in the Scottish islands peat still serves. Notice the traditionally patterned jersey.

44

42 Rural slum, 1948. In much of rural Britain in the 1920s, when agricultural depression still haunted the land, farmers and landowners could not afford to improve the often primitive conditions under which the labouring classes lived. Cottages were commonly damp, cold and totally lacking in services, and those who lived in them were on wages that did not permit much spending on comforts. Council houses were being built in villages in the early 1920s, however, and as in the 1930s farming picked up so living conditions began to improve. Vast improvements have been made since those days, and this was one of a set of photographs that in 1948 led to questions in Parliament and a new drive on rural housing. Philip Rye and his wife and six children (all under seven) had lived for six and a half years in this tin shanty at Crockenhill, Kent, one of a row of such shanties. This was not in a remote poor area but in what could be called the stockbroker belt, 25 miles from the centre of London.

43 Gipsy encampment, 1947. Gipsies have been in Britain since 1500 and a 1965 Government survey put their numbers as at least 15,000. Centrepiece in this Home Counties encampment is a Reading van, originally established by the Dunton family of Reading, Berkshire. Survivors are valuable showpieces now.

44 Gipsies being evicted, 1962. In the years since 1945 gipsies have become unpopular neighbours, constantly hounded. An increasingly tidy countryside has no place for people who do not conform, and are not notably tidy in their way of life. In this 1962 picture are car trailers, not caravans, though there is still a horse and a mule. The 1965 survey showed that only five per cent were living in horse-drawn caravans, and those mainly in the North. Since 1968 it has been a duty of local authorities to provide sites for gipsies and their location has produced as much wrangling as any other rural issue; the idea is agreed in principle but no one wants the site near them. Some authorities have set up sites and closed them again; others are still arguing about locations with residents' associations, or else just forgetting the obligation.

45 Culzean Castle, 1974. The finest Adam building in Scotland looks out over the Firth of Clyde and magnificent gardens, almost arrogant in its siting and style. Today it is the most-visited of all the Scottish National Trust's properties, with 300,000 visitors a year. The home farm has been converted into an information centre, and a busy ranger service runs a series of events to help people understand the gardens, the woods, the wild life and the country generally. After World War II a flat in the castle was placed at the disposal of General Eisenhower.

46 Butcher's shop, Oxted, Surrey, 1938. Special displays for Christmas are nothing new, but modern food regulations would not take happily to this pre-war butcher's display. Beef on the bench, poultry on the wall with a chain of sausages; pigs, more poultry and even a boar's head flanking the shop door, all make a mouth-watering display. Though multiple butchers have made inroads into the business of the old-style butcher who killed and hung his own meat, and killing now has to be done in licensed slaughter houses, there are still village butchers who buy on the hoof and do their own hanging of the meat.

47 Garage at Theale, Berkshire, 1933. Advertising signs ran riot in the 1930s, not just on garages but on every kind of shop and even the end walls of private houses. Mr Pinching's garage was photographed on this November day because he had been persuaded to discard these disfigurements. The ladders are already in place by the garage entrance and by the end of the day all were down save the main sign over the windows. In these days of one-brand petrol stations it is odd to see that three brands are on offer here, Shell, BP and National Benzole, all from hand-operated pumps.

48 Welsh chapel, 1950. Churches still play a stronger part in rural life than in the cities. This chapel at Llangower, near Bala in Wales, is 1½ miles from the nearest farm and serves a wide area but its welcoming light still shone on this December night in 1950. After taking the picture John Topham was snowed up and spent the night in his car, walking out next morning and not recovering his car till a week later.

49 Maundy peas, 1933. This charity at Sutton-at-Hone, in Kent, dating back to 1572, bound the tenant of the parsonage by his lease to give 20 bushels of peas and 2 bushels of wheat yearly to the poor of the parish. It was dispensed on Maundy Thursday: Maundy peas, the locals called it. The custom has been stopped and the charity combined with other money charities; 'Thank goodness', says the present Vicar. The old bequest had become irrelevant in modern times.

50 Rogation Sunday, 1958. Crucifer, choir, priest and congregation return to the church after blessing the fields at various corners of the village of Eynsford, Kent.

51 Almshouses, 1956. Many villages are blessed with almshouses of ancient foundation where old people can end their days in peace. In recent years the trustees of many of them have been much concerned with the lack of facilities to which the people had become accustomed but with the aid of the Charity Commissioners and the National Association of Almshouses many almshouses are now getting indoor sanitation, bathrooms and modern services. These almshouses at Aylesford, Kent, known as the Hospital of the Holy Trinity, were founded in 1605 and restored in 1842.

52   Village school on Romney
Marsh, 1949. Many village schools
were originally church foundations
and often pre-date the Education Act
of 1870 and the board schools that
followed. This school at Brenzett,
right on the edge of the open
Romney Marsh, was in 1949 also
doubling as a county library branch.
Borrowers could not come in school
time, but library officials are here
changing the books without the
children paying any attention. Behind
the pile of books, right, in the
chimney, is an old iron stove with a
brass protective rail, and behind the
male librarian is a timetable of BBC
broadcasts to schools.

53 Closing village schools. Declining rural populations have reduced the number of children in many village schools, many of which were never designed to be more than one-teacher, all-age establishments. Their numbers were further hit by putting all secondary education into large central comprehensive schools. The modern theory is that a better primary education can also be given in larger schools where children can be divided into age groups, where there is a larger staff and more facilities. The closure of village schools for these reasons has met fierce resistance, it being argued that children taken away from the villages will never work or live there. The village is further deprived of premises which often served as social centres as well. In this 1974 picture the entire population of Fulbrook School in Oxfordshire is seen outside Burford School, just a mile away across the Windrush, to which they had just been transferred and their school closed. Burford School, which is dated 1877, must be the only board school built in a Jacobean style, to match the Priory at whose gates it stands.

At Play

Through the centuries the cottagers
have spent their limited leisure in the
public houses—though the gentlemen
were not above joining them—and the
gentry and those aspiring to those
ranks have had their hunting,
shooting and fishing—which the
cottagers matched with their poaching.
In both classes the women were left
at home. Now the scope for all
increases, the social distinctions blur
a little, and the women of all ages and
classes join in or have their own
entertainments. With greater mobility
the townsman can use the countryside
for his leisure too, but this section is
concerned with the recreation of those
who live in the rural areas.

54 Skittles at the Vigo Inn, Wrotham, 1952. English public houses enjoy some forty various games, with endless local variations. This form of miniature table skittles, once common right through Kent, survives now only in the Vigo Inn at Wrotham. The board is reputedly over 150 years old and a similar aged board survives in the Horseshoes Inn, Alby, Norfolk, where the game is known as Daddlums. Every other commissioned Army officer of World War II remembers the Vigo Inn for it was the pub nearest to the wartime 'Pre-OCTU' where officer cadets had their initial training.

55 Shooting: the gamekeeper and his vermin, 1936. The leggings, corduroy breeches, game-bag and carefully broken twelve-bore all mark the experienced keeper, protecting the coops behind him in which the precious young pheasants are reared with his vermin gibbet. Jays, magpies, crows and sparrowhawks were all regarded as enemies on game preserves while the farmers shot woodpigeons, rooks, sparrows and starlings and the fishermen attacked herons, kingfishers, and cormorants. In more enlightened conservation times there is probably far less of this kind of slaughter, but this and the huge 'bags' from shoots on large estates explains the fierce opposition to shooting that exists in some quarters.

56 The Old Surrey and Burstow Hunt move off, Edenbridge, 1953. 'The unspeakable in pursuit of the uneatable' was Oscar Wilde's view of foxhunting, in which he added class distaste for the commoner disapproval of 'blood sports'. The argument that hunting is the best way of controlling the number of foxes is countered by the charge that landowners preserve foxes in order to hunt them.
But the anguish caused to most people who see a fox towards the end of its run is forgotten at the pageantry of a meet; the hunt servants in pink and the field in black, the best people in top hats, the discipline of the hounds; or by the exhilaration of hounds in full cry across the fields with the hunt streaming behind. With the modern cult of the horse the hunt has a much more democratic mix, and the majority of followers today are likely to be women. The Crown at Edenbridge is one of the few hotels in the south of England whose sign reaches right across the street.

57 Fishing, Stratford-on-Avon, 1955.
The Shakespeare industry so crowds
the birthplace of the Bard today that
placid scenes such as this are rare.
Even the Avon is much busier for it
was opened to navigation again in
1973. Apart from the dedicated fly
fishers practising their art on the
famous salmon rivers and trout
streams of Britain, there is the growing
army of coarse fishermen, mainly from
the industrial towns. Match fishing,
gambling, and increasing television
and newspaper attention have all
helped this growth, and increasingly
boys are following their elders. It is
estimated that there are nearly four
million anglers in Britain today.
In popularity it may be matched by
boating on inland waterways. As
commercial traffic died on all but a
few main canals so the waterways fell
into disuse. Today they are being
steadily opened up for pleasure
boating. The Avon navigation,
linking the Stratford canal with the
Severn, is the largest inland waterway
restoration project to be completed in
Britain.

58 Ennerdale Show, Cumbria, 1975.
Horse shows and every form of sport
and recreation concerned with horses
have huge followings today, both of
participants and spectators. Ennerdale
Show has the old traditional sports of
Lakeland as well as the fashionable
jumping events, and the lake in the
once-lonely dale has been a matter of
dispute in modern times, having been
turned like a number of the lakes
into a reservoir.

59 Cricket under Bamburgh Castle, Northumberland, 1970. Cricket is too often thought of as played by the gentlemen on soft southern greens; its popularity in fact ranges from the Isles of Scilly (a Cornish team has been a persistent winner of the Village Cricket Cup) through to these northern scenes. It is played in Scotland and Wales as well. One might suspect that association football was replacing it in modern times as the most popular team game in the country but in many areas rugby football is king. As the summer team game, cricket has no rival and it has from its recognised eighteenth-century start mixed all classes together. In this game being played on the castle lawn, however, the teams were rival rugby clubs 'looking for something to do'. Apart from one player in dark slacks everyone on the field is properly turned out: this is no unfamiliar game to them. Bamburgh Castle has a history dating back to AD 547, is one of the most conspicuous castles anywhere on the British coastline, and the village was the home of Grace Darling, the lighthouse keeper's daughter of lifeboat fame. The castle looks out across sand dunes to Holy Island.

60 Baby show, 1936. Bazaars in the winter, fetes and garden parties in the summer; these have been the village ways of raising money at least since Victorian times. At them all the baby show has always been a reliable standby. The children in this picture are plump enough for any babyfood advertisement, but the charm is in the attire of their mothers, the array of hats which would certainly be missing today, and the fact that the mothers all look much older than would their modern counterparts.

61 Combe Feast Day, Oxfordshire, 1973. Combe Feast nowadays means a two-day amusement fair on the village green and special services in the parish church, for it marks the patronal festival or the feast of the patron saint of the church, St Lawrence. Such feast days go right back into early medieval times and in past centuries have run for as long as a fortnight. Not only would the travelling entertainers come but the pedlars and wandering sellers of all kinds of goods. It was the time when villagers would buy material for new dresses, or braid, or bonnets, for the year, things that were not normally available in the village. Combe lies close to the River Evenlode and from the next village, Stonesfield, used to come the stone which was split by frost to make the distinctive roofing material of the Cotswolds. The stone has not been worked now for decades.

62 Dog Show, Guildford, 1972.
Mr T. Cass and his Old English
sheepdog wait patiently for their call
to the ring; country life would not be
complete without shows for fruits,
flowers, dogs, horses, vintage cars. . . .
Note the rig of the country gentleman;
rain-battered hat, tweed jacket, cavalry
twill slacks and strong efficient boots.

63 Crowning the May Queen, Hayes Common, Bromley, 1934. For centuries English villagers came home from the woods at crack of dawn on May Day, crowned the prettiest girl as May Queen, and crowned a May King too though his qualifications have been forgotten, danced round the Maypole and enjoyed other sports. By the mid-nineteenth century most of these customs had died out, to be revived later in the century by the schools. For decades now many London schools would select their May Queen and then on Hayes Common join in a Festival of Queens, when the Queen of London would be chosen. The festival still flourishes.

64 Folk dancing on an English tennis court, 1934. Though some mummers and Morris dance teams survived in odd villages, the old dances were disappearing in the nineteenth century along with the old songs. A Folk Song Society was started in London in 1898 to collect the music before it disappeared and Cecil Sharp, an early member, saw some Morris Men at Headington, near Oxford, the next year. He began to collect dances too, was joined by Douglas Kennedy and his wife and in 1911 the English Folk Dance Society was born. The two societies merged in 1932 and country dancing had been reborn. There are 10,000 members and nearly 600 affiliated clubs today, and in many counties the society maintains a paid organiser. Scottish country dancing has an even more enthusiastic following. The social country dancing is part of life today in many villages, and the special local dances of Morris Men, sword dancers and the like have stronger teams than ever.

65 The Rat and Sparrow Club, Eynsford, Kent, 1939. Old parish registers have innumerable entries of payments for the killing of vermin. Then the parish vestry was both church council and parish council; with the division of God and Caesar in the late nineteenth century the farmers went on paying, often through a club based on the pub: penny for a rat tail, so much for a squirrel tail, a sparrow. . . . The regular pay-out night became a competition, to see who had made most money, and then a celebratory drinking party. Here Charlie Meadows is producing his score to the treasurer of the Eynford Rat and Sparrow Club. This may not be everyone's idea of the basis for a convivial evening, but it is said that such clubs still survive.

66 The White Hart Inn, Brasted, Kent, 1965. The bar that meets present day tastes; old beams, horse brasses, open fireplace, flowers, warming pans, brightly polished furniture, stools, ice-bucket, sandwich container. By the 1930s the motor car had made the run into the country popular; women became willing to go into pubs away from their homes, and eventually into their locals. The women demanded cleanliness and cheerfulness, the 'olde-worlde inns' attracted the new trade, and the brewers made sure that the customers got what they wanted. Beams have sprouted where none existed and the old bars of some village inns are now no more than cocktail bars or ante-rooms to expensive restaurants. But by

and large pubs are better places, and in most nowadays the traveller can get good food as well. The White Hart also supports its obvious attraction with one real claim to history, it was used by some of the most famous Battle of Britain pilots in that hot summer of 1940.

67 The oldest inhabitants, the
Noah's Ark, Lurgashall, West Sussex,
1934. In spite of the strictures on
modern country pubs they can still
be found, with their local worthies
holding the best seats. Few will
match with these old men, however;
William Pannell (left) who at 78 was
still working as a hoop shaver in the
woods, and George Humphreys, still
managing his small-holding at 81.

68 Women's Institute outing,
Somerset, 1925. Since the birth of the
Women's Institute movement in
England and Wales in 1915 it has
become the largest women's
organisation in the country with
about 10,000 institutes and half a
million members, a powerful voice
in Whitehall through its national
federation and a force to be reckoned
with in most villages. It has always
been up to date and these members
of the Hinton Charterhouse (near
Bath) WI were a go-ahead lot. They
had hired a charabanc for an outing in
1925, when such things were still
novelties. Scotland has its own
federation of Women's Rural
Institutes.

69 County library mobile van, 1949. Many villages up and down Britain started their own libraries in the last century. The Public Libraries Act of 1919 permitted county councils to run village libraries, and in many counties this took the form of boxes of books in the school, with a volunteer local librarian. These became minor social centres but there were problems with maintaining a flow of books and finding librarians. After 1946 mobile libraries developed rapidly and their time of arrival became vital moments in the schedule of village life.

70 The Coronation of King George VI, 1937. The figure of the woman in the doorway and the state of the two cottages suggest no great estate or comfort, and make the cost in time and money of the decorations the more remarkable. These cottagers would have known only what the newspaper pictures and the wireless commentaries could have told them about a distant, yet obviously to them very real event. This sort of picture could have been found over and over again during the 1977 celebrations of Queen Elizabeth II's Silver Jubilee.

71 Royal Visit, Lullingstone Castle, Kent, 1936. In the country much more than in the town a royal visit is a major event. Here Queen Mary is leaving Lullingstone Castle in a Daimler as stately as herself, after having visited Lady Hart Dyke who ran a silk worm farm there from which royal wedding dresses and the clothes for royal babies were woven for so long. But the Boy Scouts and the Girl Guides are out to line the route, and all the ladies have hats on. Baden Powell, the hero of Mafeking, launched Scouting and Guiding in 1908 and, though far stronger in

urban than rural areas, they have become a part of communal life. They turn out for great occasions like the annual Remembrance Day Parade (becoming the most important of English tribal ceremonies) and have been remarkably successful in keeping abreast of the times, modernising their thinking as well as their uniforms and still the largest uniformed youth movement in Britain. The part that the Scout and Guide movement has played in teaching urban children the pleasures of the countryside has never yet been fully examined or appreciated.

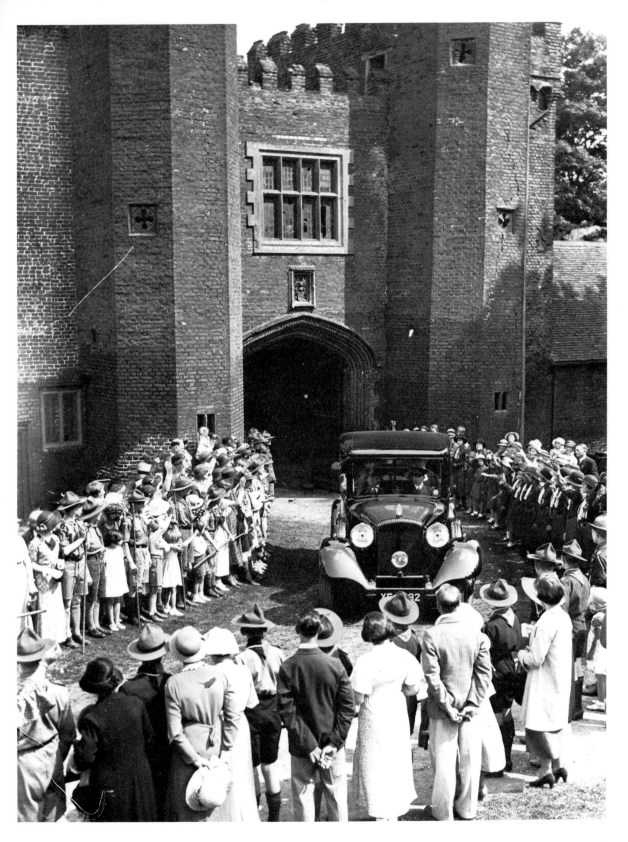

Since 1918 a variety of pressures have
put the countryside at risk. The
spread of towns is nothing new but
the pace has accelerated. The
development of road transport has
meant bigger vehicles and new roads.
Greater mobility has enabled more
townspeople to seek recreation in
rural areas. New power stations, more
industry, have all wanted land. The
total effort of two world wars brought
further strains.

72 and 73 Housing sprawl, Kent, 1930–50. These two photographs were taken from the same point but at an interval of twenty years. In the background of the left-hand picture is Gray's Farm with its oast houses, and behind the three-horse ploughing team a small urban development can just be made out. That was 1930. In the right-hand picture, taken in 1950, the London County Council's housing estate of St Paul's Cray has swept right up across the old fields. The roof line of the farm can still be made out, but the oast houses have gone.

74 Norfolk wherry and windmill, early 1920s. Railways put the canals largely out of business and in turn road transport has taken much of the freight traffic from the railways. Yet much goods traffic was carried by coastal shipping in the 1920s and 30s, and in the Thames Estuary and on the East Coast sailing barges were still busy until 1945. All this has gone under the pressure of road haulage and the Norfolk wherries, unique to the East Anglian Broads, were among the early victims. This particular craft is typical with its single gaff sail and double-ended clinker hull. In spite of the still-working windmill however and the workmanlike profile of the helmsman, its built-up topsides

and the white-bloused ladies forward suggest it may already have been converted into a pleasure boat. As a cargo carrier the barges were efficient and certainly more handsome, less of a nuisance, than the motor lorry.

75 The lorry problem, Cambridgeshire, 1974. As an increasing volume of goods traffic moved to the roads so did country areas, and above all small towns and villages, suffer. When this bridge at St Ives in Cambridgeshire was built in 1425, recesses were set over the buttresses to afford pedestrians an escape from the packhorses, but they took up less space than today's lorries —the one in the picture is small by modern standards. Such bridges suffer from the heavy loads and old buildings are not only shaken by the constant vibration of heavy vehicles, but are frequently damaged when road accidents end in the lorries actually hitting the buildings.

76 New roads, Kent, 1963. The answer to the problem of inadequate roads has been to build new ones for motor vehicles, motorways. The first stretch of M1, between London and Birmingham, was opened in 1959; this first stretch of M2 from London to Dover by-passed Rochester and Chatham. The photograph of its intersection with the Chatham-Maidstone road shows how the complex of fly-overs and link roads bites into the rural scene. A community here has been cut in two and a large area virtually reshaped. Motorways inevitably look their worst when under construction. When the earthworks have mellowed with time and the growth of vegetation they seem generally to fit into the landscape. The later ones have had more landscaping attention given them, and some stretches have the beauty of great engineering projects. But they remain intrusions, and the noise of high speed traffic is not inconsiderable.

77 Industry, Isle of Grain, 1960. More road vehicles, more factories, have all meant more oil fuel. On the estuaries of the big ports petrol refineries have been built, vast complexes like this on the Isle of Grain in Kent. These overgrown chemical works with their soaring chimneys at the top of which waste gases are burnt off can be impressive but hardly rural. To them must be added power stations with their enormous cooling towers, built on the coast or beside rivers where there is adequate water for cooling purposes, and nuclear power stations which again require large buildings and lonely sites.

78 Stonehenge, 1920. The development of flying has also brought Royal Air Force stations and civil airports into rural areas, swallowing up vast tracts of land and inflicting constant noise over many miles of country below their flight paths. In peacetime, particularly since 1946, it has been the development of civil airports that has caused most upset but in both world wars, under the cloak of national necessity, military air stations spread unchecked. In World War I when the Royal Flying Corps concentrated its development on Salisbury Plain they even built RFC Stonehenge and this 1920 picture shows how the hangars dwarfed the greatest prehistoric monument in Europe. Care for antiquities and conservation were rather novel ideas then, and it is reported that one commander of RFC Stonehenge wanted the stones pulled down because they were a nuisance to his aircraft. In the event it was the air station which disappeared. On the left of the road in the foreground stood the cottages of the Stonehenge custodians and on the right a teahouse with a small car park. Both these buildings were removed about 1936 when the National Trust acquired Stonehenge, but the rhubarb still comes up each spring in what was the custodian's garden.

79 War damage, 1940. While the bombing of World War II was mainly directed against the cities and ports, the country districts did not go unscathed. The Battle of Britain was largely fought over the fields of Kent and Sussex in 1940 and Douglas Holland's forge on Sidcup Hill was a victim. In spite of the rubble and the ruined roof, work went on, and this horse is being led in for the smith's attention.

81 Evacuees, 1940. Children evacuated from all the large towns into country areas made new rural dwellers. This group from an evacuated home all carry what was standard wear for everyone in those days, the gas mask in its awkward box.

80 Local Defence Volunteers, 1940. Countrymen and women did not escape the war; those who were not called to the Forces because their work was considered of national importance joined the Local Defence Volunteers when they were formed in 1940, before being renamed the Home Guard. Men in reserved occupations, or too old or too young for active service, all joined up; in this early parade not all the men have uniforms and the veteran in the foreground simply has an LDV armband.

82 Women's Land Army, 1946. To supplement the depleted labour force on the land women were recruited into the Land Army; this girl in the then familiar uniform of green jersey and corduroy breeches is helping at a harvest supper.

83 Sheltering from an air raid, 1940. The children of hop pickers in Kent sheltering during a raid in the Battle of Britain, 1940. Called 'the most human picture of the war', this photograph was widely circulated in the United States and was said to have played its part in bringing the Americans into the war.

84 Caravans at Prah Sands, Cornwall,
1962. Between the wars there were
townspeople establishing retreats in
near-at-hand country areas, often
do-it-yourself constructions of varying
elegance. Some became a refuge
during the bombing of World War II
and in the post-war housing shortage
continued as permanent homes. The
development of caravans for towing
behind cars after World War II
enabled townspeople seeking a modest
weekend retreat or a holiday home to
have better living accommodation but
hardly improved the scenery. A great
many of the 'mobile homes' rarely
move, though genuine touring
caravans are rapidly increasing in
numbers. These Cornish fields are
small caravan parks compared with
some in Wales and on the East Coast.

85 Youth hostellers, 1944. The
Youth Hostels Association, started in
Britain in 1930 but based on the
German pattern founded in 1914, not
only made it possible for youngsters
to use the countryside cheaply—they
paid a shilling (5p) a night for a bed—
but was also one of the many
organisations teaching a healthy
respect for the countryside. It had
nearly 300 hostels and 83,000 members
by 1939; today it has fewer hostels but
over 275,000 members and about two
million overnight stays a year. In
recent years not just walkers and
cyclists but motorists too have been
accepted.

86 Bluebell pickers, 1934. Increased mobility menaced the wild flowers of Britain until legislation, education and developing public opinion persuaded people to stop picking. These cyclists have been in bluebell woods, although all kinds of wild flowers were at risk.

87 Litter, 1920s. The increasing recreational use of the countryside has brought a litter problem. Here in the early 1920s a company of Girl Guides is clearing up a picnic site, armed with pointed sticks. The new countryside movements, youth organisations and schools did a great deal of educational work to combat litter, but it would be hard to say that the battle had yet been won.

88 Tea house, Cotesbach, Leicestershire, 1932. Catering for the increasing number of tourists has developed, not always happily, with the numbers involved. This 1930s scene is hardly crowded, with the two cyclists coping with a puncture, but the advertisements and the crude efforts of the tea house are of a kind that post war controls have thankfully removed.

89 Vintage Sports Car Club hill climb, Prescott, Gloucestershire, 1956. The motor car not only produced Britain's favourite recreational pastime, a run in the country, but also developed a sporting life of its own. Hill climbs, motor cycle trials, banger races, treasure hunts, rallies; the sport takes all forms and has in its time produced noise and nuisance which the organising authorities and clubs seek steadily to reduce. Nowadays most events, like this Prescott hill climb, are run on private roads.

90   Bird watching. One of the fastest growing and most efficient organisations of recent times has been the Royal Society for the Protection of Birds. These youngsters are on a 'sponsored bird watch' of the Young Ornithologists Club, the junior branch. Probably the birds of Britain are better protected now, and more widely observed, than any other form of wildlife.

91   Walkers on the Pennine Way, 1975. However well-intentioned the new recreational users of the countryside may be, they do damage it by their sheer weight of numbers. The Pennine Way is a footpath from the Peak District in Derbyshire to Hadrian's Wall; this southern stretch with Kinder Scout in the background shows how the very ground is worn.

92   Snowdon early 1920s. With all the pressures the wild country remains a challenge. Note the early climber on Crib Goch, his almost indolent stance and, apart from the rope about his shoulders, the every day cut of his clothes.

Chronology

1918 World War I ended November
1919 Lloyd George's Coalition Government
Board of Agriculture becomes Ministry
Forestry Commission formed
Society for Promotion of Nature Reserves (formed
  1912) acquired Wicken Fen, Cambridgeshire
1920 Cereal prices regulated by Agriculture Act,
  which put wartime measures on permanent basis
1921 Very dry year. World grain prices fell, British
  agricultural price guarantees (Corn Production Act)
  repealed, Agricultural Wages Board abolished and
  wages fell with prices
Rural Industries Bureau formed
1922 Bonar Law's Conservative Government
Wet summer. Prices slumped again
Foot-and-mouth outbreak
Summer Time Act
British Broadcasting Company began wireless
  transmission
1923 More foot-and-mouth disease
Railway companies merged into 'big four'
1924 First Labour Government. Macdonald Premier
Third wet year, more foot-and-mouth disease
County Wage Committees set up for agriculture
December, Baldwin's Conservative Government
1925 Britain back on gold standard, in effort to
  restore credit
Dartington Hall began as experiment in rural life
1926 General Strike
First outbreak in Britain of fowl pest
Norfolk Naturalists Trust formed, the pioneers
Council for the Preservation (now Protection) of
  Rural England founded
1.3m cars and motor cycles on the roads
1927 *The Countryman* magazine founded
1928 Agricultural Credits Act, making loans for
  farmers easier
1929 Macdonald's Labour Government
Crop yield above average
Agricultural land derated
Poor law administration removed from Rural District
  Councils
1930 Crops damaged by persistent rain
Youth Hostels Association formed
Road Traffic Act to control public road transport
Speed limit of 20mph for private road vehicles
  abolished

1931 Depression, National Government, Britain off
  gold standard
Poor harvest, wet weather
Agricultural Marketing Act
Land Settlement Association formed, to encourage
  small holdings
Census: population just under 45m
1932 Import Duties Act ended century of free trade
Wheat Act taxing imported grain to aid home growers
British Trust for Ornithology founded
Hikers mass trespass in Peak District
1933 Walter Elliot Minister of Agriculture
Best sunshine records of the century, crops above
  average
Milk Marketing Board established, followed by boards
  for other produce
Butlin's first holiday camp opened
1934 Drought and floods
Wheat price lowest during depression
First free milk for school children
Speed limit of 30 mph in built-up areas introduced
1935 British Sugar (Subsidy) Act, making Government
  aid for sugar beet permanent
Restriction of Ribbon Development Act
Ramblers Association formed
CPRE formed a Standing Committee on National
  Parks
Baldwin Premier
1936 King George V died. Edward VIII succeeded,
  abdicated in December
First National Forest Park, in Argyll
First television programmes broadcast by BBC
1937 King George VI crowned
Agriculture Act introduced deficiency payments for
  barley and oats, subsidies for application of lime and
  basic slag
National Veterinary Service formed
TT milk legislation
Chamberlain Premier
1938 Wheat crop exceptionally heavy
6,698 railway stations in operation
1939 Outbreak of World War II
County War Agricultural Executive Committees set up
Subsidies for ploughing up permanent grass
Less than 2.5m cars and motor cycles on roads
1940 Fall of France. Churchill replaced Chamberlain
  as Premier

1941 Combine drills began to be used in Britain
Pearl Harbor: US entered war
1942 Extremities of weather, excellent crop
1943 Good harvest
Committee for Promotion of Field Studies (later Field Studies Council), formed, beginning of field centres for environmental studies
1944 Butler's Education Act
1945 War in Europe ended
Attlee's Labour Government
Forestry Act
1946 Very wet year
Hill Farming Act
New Towns Act
National Agricultural Advisory Service set up
1947 6m sheep and 30,000 cattle died in blizzards
Tom Williams's Agricultural Act established permanent relation between state and farming
Second post-war Forestry Act aided private landowners
Town and Country Planning Act
Railways nationalised
1948 Introduction of weedkillers for cereals
1949 Nature Conservancy set up to aid wild life
National Parks and Access to the Countryside Act
Average yield of wheat 22.4cwt per acre
1950 3m cars and motor cycles on the roads
British Travel and Holidays Association formed
British agricultural output growing at 2–3 per cent, continuing until c 1965
1951 Churchill's Conservative Government
Census: population 50.25m
Forestry Act, Commission empowered to provide for amenity
1952 Queen Elizabeth II succeeded George VI
Foot-and-mouth in Scotland and anthrax (pigs) in England
1953 Myxomatosis first appeared among rabbits in England
1954 Rapid spreading of myxomatosis
Protection of Birds Act codified laws
1955 Eden Premier
1956 Ministry of Food combined with Ministry of Agriculture
1957 Macmillan Premier. D. H. Amory's Agriculture Act began to reduce guarantees
Civic Trust formed
1958 Council for Nature set up, national body of voluntary associations
Small Farmers Scheme introduced
1959 Drought in summer
1960 Rainy summer
1961 British section of World Wildlife Fund formed
1962 Free Calf Vaccination scheme against brucellosis
1963 Severe winter, considerable sheep losses

Water Resources Board set up to guide national water supplies
Beeching Report began closure of railway branch lines
Douglas-Home Premier
1964 Wilson's Labour Government
1965 Excessive rain, hay crop almost nil
1966 Winter too wet for work on land
Conservation Society formed
1967 Foot-and-mouth disease epidemic, killed over 200,000 cattle, 100,000 sheep and 100,000 pigs
Protection of Birds Act extended
Fred Peart's Agriculture Act, aid for hill farming
1968 Countryside Commission established
1969 Average yield of wheat 32.2cwt per acre
1970 Heath's Conservative Government
Over 500 nature reserves in existence
Council for Small Industries in Rural Areas created
1971 Census; Population 55.5m
Friends of the Earth formed
1972 Britain entered the European Economic Community
Dutch elm disease rampant
1973 Sandford Report on National Park policies published
50mph speed limit on roads to save petrol
1974 Wilson's Labour Government
2,357 railway stations in operation
Local government reform set up
Regional water boards began operation
Countryside Commission launched study of new agricultural landscapes
Miners' strike and three-day week in industry
1975 Act to protect wild animals and flowers
First fall in population of England and Wales since registration began in 1830s
1976 Callaghan succeeded Wilson as Premier
14m cars and motor cycles on the roads
9m elms died from Dutch elm disease
Severe drought
UK concern at spread of rabies west across Europe
1977 Severe frosts followed by much rain and flooding
Nearly 18m vehicles on roads
Silver Jubilee of Queen Elizabeth II

Index

almshouses, 54–5
Aylesford, Kent, 54–5

Bamburgh Castle, 65
Berkshire, 51
bird watching, 13, 92
blacksmiths, 30, 84
Boy Scouts, 75
Brasted, Kent, 71
Brenzett, Romney Marsh, 56
Burford, Oxfordshire, 57

Cambridgeshire, 79
Canterbury market, 32
caravans, 28, 46, 47, 88
Carlisle hiring fair, 17
carting, 37
cattle ranching, 25
chair bodgers' camp, 28
chapels, 52
charcoal burning, 28
charities, 52, 54–5
Chiddingstone, Kent, 41
Chipping Campden, 14–15
churches, 11, 14–15, 40, 52, 53
Cirencester, 40
Civic Trust, 13, 40
climbing, 93
Combe Feast Day, Oxfordshire, 66
conservation, 12–13
Cornwall, 29, 88
Coronation, George VI, 74
Cotesbach, Leicestershire, 91
Cotswolds, 14–15, 40
Council for the Preservation of Rural
England, 12
Council for Small Industries in Rural Areas
(CoSIRA), 31
Countryside Commission, 9, 13
Court Farm, Chipping Campden, 14–15
cricket, 65
Crowther, F., railway porter, 33
cultivating, 10, 19, 76
Culzean Castle, 48–9
Cycling, 11, 89

dairying, 24
Dean Bottom, Kent, 44
Department of the Environment, 13
donkeys, carrying milk, 18

Edenbridge, Kent, 61
education, 11, 56, 57
Ennerdale Show, 64
evacuees, 85
Exmoor, 8
Eynsford, Kent, 53, 70

Fair Isle, 18
fairs, 17, 66
fishing, 62–3
folk dancing, 69
forestry, 11, 12, 13, 25

gamekeeping, 60
Girl Guides, 75, 90
Gloucestershire, 14–15, 40
Goldup, Fred, 17

Groombridge, Sussex, 30
Gypsies, 46, 47

Hall Court, Much Marcle, 21
Hampshire, 24
harvesting, 8, 10, 17, 20, 21, 22, 26
Hayes Common, Bromley, 68
hedges, destruction of, 8
Hemingford Abbots, Huntingdon, 31
Herefordshire, 21
Highlands, Scottish, 25
hill climb, 91
Hobhouse Report (1947), 8–9
Home Guard, 84–5
hop-picking, 27, 87
horses, 8, 14, 19, 20, 36, 37, 40, 61, 64, 76
housing sprawl, 76–7
Humphreys, George, Lurgashall, 72
Hunting, 61
Huntingdonshire, 31

Isle of Grain, 82

Kent, 26, 32, 41, 45, 52, 54–5, 61, 68, 70, 71,
75, 76–7, 80–1, 82–3, 87

Lacock, Wiltshire, 9
Lake District, 8, 12, 64
Lanarkshire, 23
Lanesfoot Farm, Troutbeck, 8
Leicestershire, 91
Leslie, William, Fair Isle, 18
libraries, 56, 73
Lincolnshire, 26
litter, 90
living standards, 9, 10–11, 12, 38–9, 42–7
Lullingstone Castle, Kent, 75

MacDonald, Donald, North Uist, 36
Malcolmson, Mrs, Lerwick, 44
markets, 32
Mastiles Lane, 11
May Day, 68
Meadows, Charlie, Eynsford, Kent, 70
Middle Woodford, Wiltshire, 22
Middleton in Teesdale station, 33
milk carrying, 18
mills, 35, 78
motor car, 9–10, 30, 34, 51
motorways, 80–1
Munday, Rebecca, Dean Bottom, Kent, 44

Naseby, Northamptonshire, 16
national parks, 9, 12–13
National Trust, 11, 14, 35, 41, 48–9
navigations, 35, 63
Nettlestead Farm, Paddock Wood, 27
Newark Mill, Surrey, 35
Norfolk, 58–9, 78
Norfolk wherry, 78
North, Jim, Paddock Wood, 27
Northamptonshire, 16
Northumberland, 65

ox cart, 18
Oxfordshire, 57, 62–3, 66

Oxted, Surrey, 50
Outer Hebrides, 36

Pannell, William, Lurgashall, 72
peat carrying, 44
Pennine Way, 92
ploughing, 19, 37
police, 11
postmen, 18, 27, 36
poultry, 26
Prah Sands, Cornwall, 88
public houses, 58–9, 70, 71, 72

railways, 33
Ramblers' Association, 12, 42
roads, 34, 76–7, 79, 80–1
Romney Marsh, 56
Rural Industries Bureau, 31
Rural Industries Loan Fund, 31
Rye, Philip and family, Crockenhill, 45

St Ives, Cambridgeshire, 79
St Paul's Cray, 77
Scotland, 23, 26, 36, 44, 48–9
Seaman, O., Godmanchester, 31
sheep, 23
Shetland, 44
shopping, 10, 51
shows, 64, 66, 67
Sidcup Hill, 84
slums, rural, 45
Snowdonia, 8, 93
Somerset, 73
South Downs, 9, 10
steam in agriculture, 19
Stonehenge, 83
Stratford-on-Avon, 62–3
Surrey, 35, 51, 67
Sussex, 30–1, 43, 72

table skittles, 58–9
thatching, 31
Theale, Berkshire, 51
Thomson, Bob, Troutbeck, 8
Timberton Bottom, 42
tithe barn, 16

vermin catching, 14, 60, 70
Vigo Inn, Wrotham, 59

waggons, 14–15
Wales, 8, 52, 93
walking, 12, 42, 92
wartime, 21, 43, 59, 71, 83, 84–7
water supply, 44
welfare state, 10–11, 12
wheelwright, 29
wildflower protection, 89
Williams, J. C., Mawgan in Meneage, 29
Wiltshire, 22, 83
women, in agriculture, 26, 86
Women's Institute, 73
Women's Land Army, 86

Yorkshire, 11, 18, 33, 34
Youth Hostels Association, 12, 89